A Kid's Summer EcoJournal

With Nature Activities for Exploring the Season

Toni Albert

Designed and Illustrated by
Margaret Brandt

Trickle Creek Books
"Teaching Kids to Care for the Earth"

Tel: 717-766-2638 • 800-353-2791 • Fax: 717-766-134.

www.TrickleCreekBooks.com

D1275195

Author's Acknowledgments

Thank you, Bob Albert, for our home at Trickle Creek,
for clearing the land and building the house with your own hands,
for long happy walks in the woods, and long happy days together.
Thank you for supporting me in every way!

Thank you, Pat Van Etten, for being the best of business partners.
We have learned so much together.

Thank you, Margaret, for letting your love of nature
shine through every beautiful page of art.

Artist's Acknowledgments

I'd like to dedicate this art to the summer days of childhood spent exploring
the lush woodlands, streams, and fields with friends, both human and furry.

Thank you, Clarke Slade, for all your understanding, love, and support
through the many long days spent illustrating these pages.

Dedication

To all the children who love summer days and use them to explore
the strange and wonderful wildernesses in backyards.
To Nathan and Kayla, the first grandchildren in our family, and to future grandbabies!

First printing 1998, Second printing 2005

Publisher's Cataloging in Publication
(Prepared by Quality Books Inc.)

Albert, Toni.
A kid's summer ecojournal : with nature activities for
exploring the seasons / Toni Albert; illustrated and designed
by Margaret Brandt.
p. cm.
SUMMARY: Includes tips on writing about nature, short
entries from the author's nature journal, and nature activities for
exploring the season.
Preassigned LCCN: 96-61930
ISBN-13: 9780964074248
ISBN-10: 0-9640742-4-9
1. Nature study—Juvenile literature. 2. Natural history—
Juvenile literature. 3. Ecology—Juvenile literature. 4. Spring—
Juvenile literature. 5. Diaries—Authorship—Juvenile literature.
I. Title.

QH48.A53 1998   574.5'43
QB197-40114

Published in the United States by Trickle Creek Books
500 Andersontown Road, Mechanicsburg, PA 17055

Contents

4 Introduction: Writing About Nature

5 Introduction: Exploring Nature

6 Summer EcoJournal: June 1

7 Trickle Creek
Make a map of the place you observe.

8 Summer EcoJournal: June 3

9 Summer Hummers
Make a hummingbird feeder.

10 Summer EcoJournal: June 4

11 Grow a Giant Sunflower
Grow a huge flower and harvest the seeds.

12 Summer EcoJournal: June 8

13 Make a Sun Print
Be creative with the sun.

14 Summer EcoJournal: June 9

15 Make a Sun Cooker
Bake a potato with heat from the sun.

16 Summer EcoJournal: June 13

17 Build Something for a Turtle
Make a turtle loafing platform.

18 Summer EcoJournal: June 18

19 Tiny Lanterns in the Grass
Collect grasses—and fireflies.

20 Summer EcoJournal: June 20

21 Search for Salamanders
How to find and keep a salamander.

22 Summer EcoJournal: June 30

23 How to Tail a Snail
Do experiments with snails.

24 Summer EcoJournal: July 5

25 How to Track and Capture BUGS
Be a big bug buff.

26 Summer EcoJournal: July 8

27 Explore a Pond
Explore the mysteries of a lively pond.

28 Summer EcoJournal: July 11

29 Grow a Gourd House for a Bird
How to grow a birdhouse.

30 Summer EcoJournal: July 16

31 Creek Critters
Collect crazy creek critters.

32 Summer EcoJournal: July 17

33 Keep a Creek Aquarium
How to keep crazy creek critters cozy.

34 Summer EcoJournal: July 18

35 Make Sun Tea and Mint Lemonade
When the livin' is easy.

36 Summer EcoJournal: July 22

37 Plan a Low-Trash Picnic
Have lunch without litter.

38 Summer EcoJournal: July 25

39 Attract Moths with a Shining Sheet
Observe gorgeous little creatures of night.

40 Summer EcoJournal: August 1

41 You Can Be a Bee
Pollinate flowers with a paintbrush.

42 Summer EcoJournal: August 6

43 Help a Sloppy Mourner
Make a nest cone for mourning doves.

44 Summer EcoJournal: August 15

45 Make a Mushroom Spore Print
How to make an unusual print.

46 Summer EcoJournal: August 20

47 Birds in Summer
Make a dust bowl. Collect bird eggshells.

48 Summer EcoJournal: August 24

49 Safari to a World of Tiny Monsters
Visit an unearthly world by magnifying it.

50 Summer EcoJournal: August 28

51 When You Know a Tree
How to study a tree and gain a friend.

52 Summer EcoJournal: August 31

53 Celebrate Summer
You know what to do!

54 Wildlife Checklist

55 Summer Butterflies

56 An EcoJournal for Every Season

Introduction
Writing About Nature

Summer days stretch out long like a lazy cat or a comet's tail or a frog's tongue. In summer, there is time to lie in the grass and peer at unearthly insects, time to wade in a creek and catch minnows, time to sleep in the sun. Even at the end of day, there is still time to play in the dark, guided by starlight and tiny firefly lanterns. In summer, away from the pressure of school assignments, you can write for your own enjoyment. You can keep a summer-long eco-journal.

What should you write in your eco-journal?
Anything about nature....

- Write daily notes about the way the season progresses. This takes careful observation. For example, did you ever notice when the wild roses bloom or when the nightly "bug buzz" concert starts?

- Write a poem, a story, or an essay. Draw inspiration from the sweet smell of summer rain, the taste of fat juicy blackberries, or the sight of a lazy turtle on a log. Express your thoughts and feelings about nature.

- Make quick field notes when you are observing something outside. Record details that you may forget later—the color of a mushroom, the shape of a leaf, the pattern on a frog, the activity of an insect. Field notes often include the date and time, the weather, and the location, as well as a description of what you were observing and what happened to it while you were watching. (You can make quick drawings, too.)

- Use your field notes to write a careful description of what you observed. Use detailed, descriptive language.

- Keep a record of an interesting nature study or experiment, such as tracking insects, growing a sunflower, or keeping a creek aquarium.

- Write an interview with a park ranger, a wildlife rehabilitator, a zookeeper, or someone who knows something special about wildlife or wildlands.

- Write a report about an animal or plant that interests you.

- Keep a nature diary with descriptions of special events, such as seeing a fawn with its mother or watching a bird take a dust bath.

- Read a book about nature. Then write your response.

Keeping an eco-journal will give you a chance to write from your own direct experience. (And writing based on experience is often your best writing.) It is easy to draw inspiration from nature. As you write in your eco-journal, you may find yourself painting word pictures and making your writing sound like poetry. Writing about nature will help you learn to be more observant and to enjoy nature more, too.

Exploring Nature

It's fun to run through a field of tall grass, scramble up rocks, crash through the underbrush, or splash in a creek. But that's not the best way to see wildlife. You need to learn to enter the quiet world of animals and plants slowly and gently without disturbing them. You must practice being still—but with all your senses alert. You must become observant and more observant and more and more observant! Then you'll see a fawn in the sun-dappled woods. Or spot the first firefly of summer. Or discover a toad burrowed in a flowerpot. It takes patience and skill to explore nature, but the delight of discovery and the joy of caring for our earth will last all of your life.

Here are some tips for exploring nature:

- Wear long pants, a long-sleeved shirt, and sturdy shoes. Wear greens and browns.

- Be prepared. Bring drinking water, bug spray, plastic containers for collecting specimens, a magnifying lens, and a notebook and pencil. If you have a camera, binoculars, or field guides, bring them, too. Bring a small trash bag for litter.

- Look for animals at dawn or dusk. That's when you will be most likely to see them.

- Move quietly. Sit still in one place for awhile—at least five minutes. Hide partly behind a tree or boulder. Try to feel like a part of nature.

- Watch where you step (don't step on a snake!) and don't put your hands into hollow logs or trees before you look inside.

- Use all of your senses. Listen to the sounds around you. Breathe deeply and notice different smells. Look around you and observe details. Touch the bark of trees, fuzzy moss, smooth stones in a creek. Taste edible plants and berries *only* when an adult gives you permission. (Some plants are poisonous.) Don't forget to use your sense of wonder, too!

- Look for signs of wildlife: animal tracks, animal trails, burrows, nests, feathers or fur, owl pellets, bones, droppings, and evidence that animals have eaten or grazed (squirrels drop nutshells, rabbits strip leaves from small plants, birds take berries from bushes).

- If you see an animal and want to get closer, don't approach it directly. Take a roundabout route, walking slowly and steadily. Don't look the animal in the eye or you will alarm it. The best way to get a closer look at an animal is with binoculars.

- Stay on a path or marked trail. Then you won't get lost and you won't trample delicate plants or animal nests.

- Always leave an area as clean as you found it—or cleaner. When you leave, carry trash out with you. Replace any rocks or logs you overturned as you looked for tiny wildlife.

Special tips on water safety:

- NEVER explore in or near water alone. Make sure an adult knows where you are. Wear a life jacket when you investigate a pond or creek. There may be unexpected deep pools or white water. Wear sneakers to protect your feet. Don't pick up a water creature with your hands. It might bite or sting, and you might hurt it, too.

Summer EcoJournal

June 1: Trickle Creek is where I live with my husband Bob, our dog Abercrombie, and our white cat, Bailey. Our twenty acres is a miniature wildland brimming with wildlife—a perfect place to explore nature. There is a deep woods, a wildflower meadow, a large pond, and the tiny creek that we call Trickle Creek.

Today we had visitors who have never been here before, friends from out of town. We were sitting at the kitchen table, chatting and watching two blue jays at the feeder, when a raccoon came boldly out of the woods. It climbed into the deer feeder and calmly ate shelled corn with its dainty hands while we watched with wide eyes. A few moments later, a sleek red-haired doe approached the feeder. Without hesitating, she pushed her muzzle into the corn and lazily chewed, as if she saw nothing strange about eating from a feeder with a raccoon in it! Next a gray squirrel came down from a nearby tree and settled under the feeder—and under the raccoon—to pick up dropped kernels of corn.

Our friends were amazed, but no more amazed than we were. After they left, I asked, "Do you think we overdid the wildlife show? Are we starting to live in a Disney movie?" We stared at each other and nodded and laughed.

6

Trickle Creek

Kids look forward to long summer days of vacation. Time stretches out like lazy waves of heat. There is time to lie on your back and watch clouds sail overhead. Or explore the mysteries of a pond. Or grow a sunflower and drink sun tea. After dark, there are fireflies to catch and moths to attract and crickets to stalk. Summer is a magical time to explore nature.

One of the best ways to learn about nature—and start to really care about it—is to visit the same place over and over until you know it by heart. The place can be your backyard or school yard, a vacant lot or city park, a nature trail or country path, or even a single tree rising above city pavement. It's fun to make a map or drawing—perhaps a view from the air—of the place you choose to observe. You can make notes on your drawing to keep track of seasonal changes, wildlife sightings, and sources of water, food, and shelter for wildlife. It's fun to add sketches, too. Then you'll have a special record of summer discoveries.

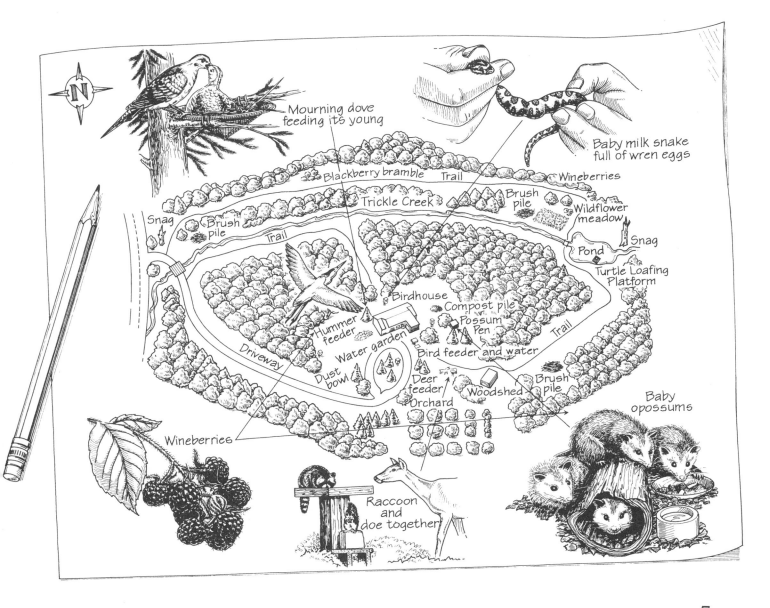

Summer EcoJournal

June 3: Today we saw the raccoon again, but this time I wasn't happy to see it. In summer, we eat almost every meal outside. Our favorite place is at the end of the deck where we feed the hummingbirds. It's a delight to watch a tiny hummer maneuver like a miniature helicopter. The little bird approaches the feeder, hovers over the target, dives in with its needlelike beak, and then backs out—all without landing. We can *hear* this little helicopter, too. Its wings beat at just the right range to produce a low humming sound. We love the hummers. We keep their feeder filled with sugar water, a kind of homemade nectar, so that they will keep us company while we picnic.

When we carried our lunch outside at noon, we surprised the raccoon robbing the hummingbird feeder. The raccoon had climbed out on a tree limb and had pulled the feeder down. It was drinking the sugar water with eager slurps. Its facial markings, a black bandit's mask, made it look like the clever, mischievous thief it is. When we glimpsed its belly, the swollen nipples told us that the raccoon is a nursing mother. No wonder she is eating the deer's corn and drinking the hummer's nectar. She has little black-masked bandits to feed!

Summer Hummers

Would you like to invite the smallest bird in the world to visit your backyard or school yard? Would you like to watch a tiny bird like a shimmering jewel, with invisible wings that beat at fifty beats per second? Would you like to make friends with a hummingbird?

Seeds and water will attract many birds, but hummingbirds, or "hummers," must have flowers. And their favorite flowers are red. If you plant nectar-filled flowers, especially tube-shaped flowers, and especially *red* flowers, any hummers in the area will surely want to spend the summer with you! Trumpet vines, columbines, morning-glories, lilies, honeysuckles, impatiens flowers, jewel weeds, nasturtiums, petunias, coral bells, snapdragons, and bee balms are some of the flowers that attract hummers and give them instant energy. The little birds sip nectar from the flowers with their long needlelike bills. They also eat tiny insects from the flowers.

It's fun to feed hummers sugar water in special hummingbird feeders, but it's important that the birds also have natural food—flower nectar and insects. Then they have a proper diet to keep up their rapid darting, hovering, and hurrying, and to feed the baby hummers what they need. You can buy feeders. (Make sure you buy one that can be taken apart and cleaned often.) Or you can easily make a feeder. Insert the stopper and tube from a small-animal water bottle into the spout of a plastic bottle. Choose a red bottle, or cut a red plastic flower that can slip over the tube. Or simply use the water bottle as a hummingbird feeder. You can also hang a glass jar at a 45- degree angle from a tree or post. Fill your feeder with homemade hummingbird nectar. Clean the feeder and replace the nectar every three or four days.

Recipe for Hummingbird Nectar

1 part granulated sugar
4 parts water

Combine the sugar and water in a small pan. Have an adult help you bring it to a boil over high heat. Remove it from the heat and let it cool. You can store leftover nectar in the refrigerator for a week. (Don't add food coloring. Add red to the feeder itself.)

tilted glass jar

plastic bottle
stopper
tube
red plastic

The 3-inch ruby-throated hummingbird migrates 500 miles across the Gulf of Mexico without stopping.

Summer EcoJournal

_____

_____

_____

_____

_____

_____

_____

_____

June 4: Bob found the raccoon's den! As he was walking in the woods not far from our house, he spotted the raccoon in the branches of an old tree. There is a big hole in the tree about six feet off the ground where a large limb broke off. He saw two little raccoon faces peeking out of the cavity.

Of course, I wanted to see the den, too. I followed Bob to the den tree, but there were no raccoons in sight. I walked quietly to the base of the tree and put my ear against it. I could hear scratching and shuffling and little grunts and soft chirping-purring sounds inside! Bob lifted me up, so that I could look in, and there they were—five sleepy raccoon cubs cuddled together for a nap. They opened their eyes and stared sleepily at me. There was some shifting of position. One little animal crawled over the others to settle on top. One burrowed deeper. Their hair is soft and downy like the wispy feathers of a baby bird or the downy hair of a puppy. Each small face is perfectly masked. Their mother wasn't with them, but I knew she could be watching us from somewhere nearby. We only stayed a minute, not wanting to disturb her *too* much.

Walking back through the sparkling light and deep green shadows of the woods, I thought what a beautiful home those raccoon bandits have. The delicate wild roses are still blooming in great, glorious clumps. Their tiny pink and white petals are like the little shells you find on the beach, and their fragrance is like bottled summer. It probably won't be long before the coon cubs will leave their cozy den and start exploring. What will we be in for then?

10

Grow a Giant Sunflower

Hot summer days are the perfect time to grow giant sunflowers, which may look down on you from twice your height. Their foot-wide faces are fringed with bright yellow petals like rays from the sun. It's so much fun to grow these sunny giants—just to see how big they get! But there is another benefit. Sunflower seeds are tasty and nutritious for people and animals alike.

Sunflowers need lots of sun, plant food, water, and room to grow. Prepare the soil in a large sunny area by mixing it with compost if you have it. (*Note: Directions for making compost are given in* A Kid's Fall EcoJournal. *See page 56 for information about how to get the Fall EcoJournal.*) Plant several sunflower seeds one-half inch deep and about one foot apart. Water the seeds with liquid fertilizer or with plant food dissolved in water. The seeds should sprout in one to two weeks.

Give the sunflower plants plenty of water and more plant food as they grow. Measure the plants every week and record their growth. (You might want to make drawings or take photos, too.) When the sunflowers grow big and heavy with seeds, you may have to support the flower heads by gently tying them to stakes driven into the ground. Or sometimes you can carefully loop two or three plants together to support each other. When the flowers fade and begin to drop their petals—and when birds begin to pick at the outer rows of seeds—it is time to cut the flowers. Cut them on a dry, hot afternoon, and leave about a foot of stem. Then you can hang the flowers upside down to dry.

When the sunflower seeds are good and dry, they will pop out of the flower head when you lightly rub your finger across it. Catch the seeds in a paper bag. If you store them in an airtight container, they will keep for a long time. You can put them out for birds, squirrels, chipmunks, mice, and moles. Or roast them in a 300-degree oven on a cookie sheet for ten to fifteen minutes and eat them yourself!

Sunflowers are fun-flowers!

Summer EcoJournal

_____

_____

_____

_____

_____

_____

_____

_____

_____

June 8: Every day, we put our food scraps and yard trimmings on a compost pile. The idea is to make *compost*, a rich, soil-like mixture that is good for all kinds of plants. But since our compost pile is at the edge of the woods, it's really more like a feeding station for small animals. They come and go all night, sometimes eating on top of the pile, sometimes dragging food into the woods. There are narrow animal trails, worn by nightly forages to the compost pile, which come from three directions.

After dark, we check the compost pile by turning on an outdoor light. Then we can watch them through the windows. Last night I saw a fat baby opossum with its nose in the air, shuffling first in one direction, then in another, following the scent of food. Opossums have weak eyes but good noses. The little animal had almost reached its goal, when a red fox appeared. The fox trotted toward the pile, alert and wary, looking over its shoulder. The opossum turned around and lumbered straight into the shelter of the woods. I thought the fox had been attracted by chicken skin from our dinner, but it chose a watermelon rind and carried it jauntily away.

I got to know some baby possums once when my daughter-in-law, Terri, asked me to keep four of them until they were big enough to be released. Terri's grandmother had called the police, because she thought there were four rats in her kitchen. The police obligingly caught the "rats," explained that they were little possums, and offered to destroy them. That's when Terri stepped in. She got permission from the Humane Society to care for them and brought them to me.

What a gift!

Make a Sun Print

All you need to make beautiful nature prints are bright sunlight and sun print paper. You can buy sun print paper or a sun print kit in nature stores and educational toy stores. A sun print kit usually includes a sheet of clear acrylic the same size as the sheets of sun print paper. You will also need a shallow pan of water for this project.

On a bright sunny summer day, place a sheet of sun print paper, blue side up, on a flat surface outside in direct sunlight. To make a nature print, immediately put a natural object—for example, a wildflower, a fern, a feather, or a thin twig with leaves—on the paper. Press the object flat by covering it with a sheet of clear acrylic. Leave the object in place until the paper fades and the paper under the object turns dark. It will take about five to ten minutes. Then soak the paper in water in a shallow pan for another two minutes. The dark print will become white and the paper will darken. Finally, lay the paper flat and let it dry. You have made a sun print!

Try making more complicated designs by arranging objects on a plain sheet of paper before moving them to the sun print paper. Experiment by adding objects to the sun print paper at different times. For example, make an interesting leaf print by adding another leaf every minute for five minutes while the sun print is being made. You might want to add letters cut from paper to make words on your sun print. See how creative you and the sun can be!

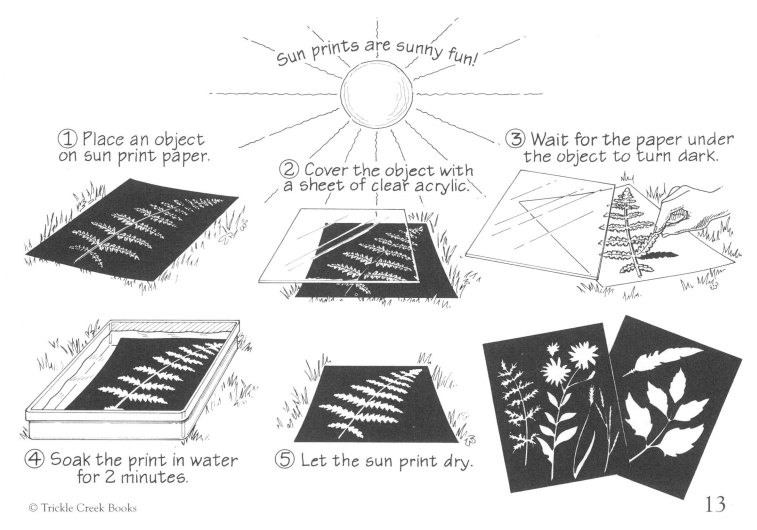

Sun prints are sunny fun!

① Place an object on sun print paper.

② Cover the object with a sheet of clear acrylic.

③ Wait for the paper under the object to turn dark.

④ Soak the print in water for 2 minutes.

⑤ Let the sun print dry.

Summer EcoJournal

_____

_____

_____

_____

_____

_____

_____

_____

June 9 (*Baby possums' story continued*): The little possums were about *half* cute with their pointed snouts, tiny sharp teeth, and long hairless, scaly tails. We kept them in a dog's travel kennel equipped with a small hollow log, where they slept. They were messy. They spilled their food and walked in it—and walked in other messes they made, too. I wasn't at all sure that I was meant to be an opossum's mother.

When the possums were about five inches long, not counting their rat tails, I called the Humane Society to ask if it was time to release them. I was ready. I was told that we should keep them for several more months in a larger cage where they could climb. When I asked Bob to build a big possum cage, he said flatly, "No." But later that day, I heard hammering, and the next day we moved the opossums into their new home.

The wire-mesh cage was five feet high and three feet wide with a sturdy roof. We wired several branches, almost little trees, inside the cage, and I added a pile of dogwood branches to serve as cover for the young animals. Opossums are not noted for being very intelligent. And I had lost all respect for them after seeing how messy they were. So I was amazed to see the baby possums use the dogwood leaves and branches to build a cozy nest for themselves. They proved to be skilled climbers, too, pulling themselves hand over hand to the top of the cage. They used their tails as another hand, even hanging by their tails. Since the floor of the cage was dirt, I no longer had to clean up after them, and in a more natural environment, they kept themselves clean. We enjoyed the rest of their stay with us, and Abercrombie, who spent long, fascinated hours watching them, probably missed them when they left.

Make a Sun Cooker

Have you ever heard someone say, "It's so hot you could fry an egg on the sidewalk"? Did you ever think of trying it? Many people have experimented with finding ways to cook with heat from the sun. The key to success is to build a sun cooker that reflects the rays of the sun and concentrates heat on the food that needs to be cooked.

You can make a bowl into an efficient sun cooker. Find a bowl with as small a base as possible. If you have an aluminum bowl, polish the inside of the bowl until it is smooth and shiny. That will make a bright surface that will reflect the sun rays. If your bowl is not aluminum, you can line it with aluminum foil. Make sure the dull side of the foil is against the inside of the bowl. Your job is to make the foil-covered bowl as smooth and shiny as possible. Smooth the foil with the back of a large spoon, or roll a rubber ball over the foil to remove every wrinkle. Try to make the bowl as bright as a mirror.

To cook a small potato, first place a little suction hook inside the bowl at the bottom. (Straighten the hook with pliers to form a spike.) If you're working with an aluminum bowl, simply attach the suction hook directly to the bottom of the bowl. But if you have a foil-covered bowl, open a small slit in the foil, so that you can attach the suction hook to the surface of the bowl. Place the potato securely on the suction hook. Take the sun cooker outside at noontime when the sun is hottest, and point it directly at the sun. As the sun moves lower in the sky, change the position of the bowl so that the sun shines directly into it. Check the potato with a fork. When the fork slips easily into the potato, it is done! How long did it take? What else could you cook in a sun cooker?

Be careful! A sun cooker gets hot and so does a cooked potato!

An easy way to position the bowl is to place it in sand.

These few materials will make a sun cooker.

Suction Hook

Hook straightened into spike

Graham Crackers

CHOCOLATE CHIPS

Aluminum Foil

Summer EcoJournal

_____

_____

_____

_____

_____

_____

_____

_____

_____

June 13: Several years ago, Bob and I hired a bulldozer to dig a large pond in a clearing in the woods. Trickle Creek, which begins as a spring, flowed into the basin of the pond and filled it with fresh, clear spring water. We planted some cattails and stocked the pond with bass and bluefish. Then we watched to see how this pond ecosystem would develop. Today the pond brims with wildlife. How did turtles and frogs and diving beetles and duckweed find their way to this secret water place? It amazes me.

As I approached the pond early this morning, I tried to walk slowly and quietly, being especially observant. I know from experience that you have to sneak up on a pond. Otherwise, ducks will rise into the air with a clatter of wings, deer will crash into the underbrush with their magnificent white tails bushed up, turtles will slide off logs and disappear underwater, frogs will hop and plop into weeds in the shallows, and minnows and tadpoles will hide under soggy leaves and rocks. All you'll see will be bright blue and green dragonflies and still water.

Sneaking toward the pond, I heard the voice of a bullfrog, a deep, twangy note like a plucked banjo string. A smaller frog sat on the turtle loafing platform that we put out last year, and a painted turtle sunned itself at the very edge of the water. The turtle slipped into the water without a ripple. I saw a big brown water spider perched on top of the water near a patch of delicate duckweed. Daisies are blooming on the sunny bank of the pond, and there is a spiky, purple wildflower that I've never seen before. But best of all, I saw tiny, dainty hoofprints among the deer tracks leading to the water. The fawns are born and they are in this very woods!

16

Build Something for a Turtle

Even a small pond is a rich habitat for animals and plants. The shallow water at the edge of a pond is a fascinating place to explore. Approach the pond very slowly and quietly, so that your sudden reflection in the water or the vibration of your footsteps don't disturb turtles, frogs, or snakes basking in the sun. See if you can reach the water without frightening away the minnows, water beetles and other insects, tadpoles, and salamanders that enjoy the shallows. This is hard to do. You'll have to practice sneaking up on a pond!

Turtles, the most intelligent reptiles, are especially hard to sneak up on. As soon as they sense your presence, they quickly slip off the logs or rocks where they sun themselves. But if you sit down and stay still and quiet, you may see a turtle cautiously lift its head out of the water and eventually climb back on its log or rock. Look carefully at the shape, size, markings, and colors of the turtle, so that later you can identify it in a field guide. My favorite pond turtle is the painted turtle, because of its gorgeous red and yellow markings on a polished olive-green shell. My least favorite water turtle is the snapping turtle. A snapper is a mean predator that will eat baby ducks, frogs, salamanders, snakes, and even other turtles. On land, a snapping turtle will lunge at a person. It is good advice to leave snapping turtles alone.

You can easily build a loafing platform for turtles. (Other animals will use it too.) You'll need three cedar logs—24 inches long and about 4 inches in diameter—and four 2-inch-by-6-inch-by-24-inch spruce boards. Lay the logs side by side with about 6 inches between them. Then lay the boards across the logs and nail them in place with 16 penny common nails. Space the boards about ½ inch apart. Float the loafing platform in 2 to 4 feet of water in a sunny part of a pond. Tie one end of a nylon rope to the loafing platform and tie the other end to half of a heavy concrete block. Drop the block below the platform to anchor it. Now you can practice sneaking up on the loafing platform to see which animals enjoy it.

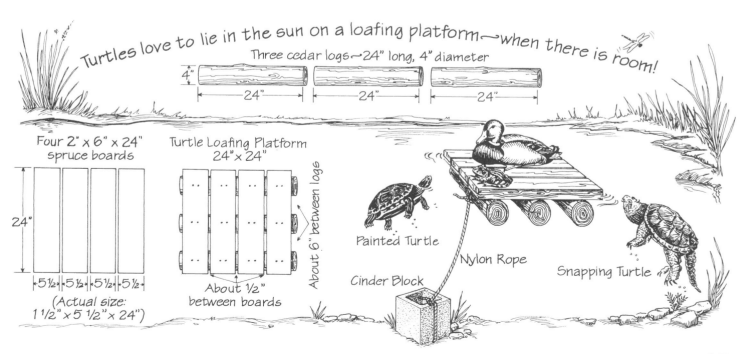

Turtles love to lie in the sun on a loafing platform—when there is room!

Three cedar logs—24" long, 4" diameter

4"

24" 24" 24"

Four 2" x 6" x 24" spruce boards

Turtle Loafing Platform 24" x 24"

24"

5½ 5½ 5½ 5½

(Actual size: 1 ½" x 5 ½" x 24")

About ½" between boards

About 6" between logs

Painted Turtle

Cinder Block

Nylon Rope

Snapping Turtle

Summer EcoJournal

_____
_____
_____
_____
_____
_____
_____
_____
_____
_____

June 18: Today I took a favorite walk beside a wetland meadow about a mile from here. The grasses in the meadow are tall and lush. From a distance, the wetland is a feathery, purple haze of color. Up close, there are almost a dozen different grasses, some with coarse, grain-like tops and others as delicate as colored thread. I cut a bouquet of wild grasses with a small pair of garden shears. I'll give them to Margaret, the illustrator of this book, so that she can include them in the art.

The meadow grasses smell good—and sound good, too. They whisper and rustle and echo with insect calls. Large patches of small lavender thistles are covered with white butterflies and other insects. I always see wild canaries (goldfinches) in this open area. The male is bright yellow with black wings. He darts up and down, here and there, like a black and yellow butterfly.

I passed the "snake tree," where I often see a black snake curled up in a small hollow in the trunk. It never moves as I walk by. I've even stopped to look at the snake more closely without alarming it. It probably would have alarmed me if I had known how big it was. One day when the snake wasn't in its tree, I saw a long snakeskin hanging out of the tree cavity. I pulled it carefully out of the tree without tearing it. The snakeskin was four feet long! The snake must have shed its skin not long before I found it, because it was perfect in every detail. The shape of the head, the texture of the body, the fine narrow tail were all preserved exactly.

18

Tiny Lanterns in the Grass

Grasses cover the earth. Some kind of grass can be found almost anywhere, even on rocky ground, arid desert, or arctic tundra. Even at the bottom of a pond or in the shallow grass beds of the sea. Even between the cracks in a sidewalk. You probably take grass for granted. You probably walk right on it! But once you begin to really notice wild grasses, you may appreciate them in a new way.

In summer, when wild grasses flower, they add delicate colors and beautiful forms to fields, meadows, roadsides, and "lawnsides." (All grasses have flowers, but the flowers don't have petals. They have leaflike *bracts*, which look like tiny scales at the tops of the stems.) There are more than 1200 native species of grass in North America. You should be able to find ten to twenty different grass species in a typical low-lying meadow. See how many you can collect. They are easy to preserve. Simply tie the stems together and hang the grasses upside down to dry.

Birds, squirrels, chipmunks, mice, and raccoons, among other animals, eat the seeds and grains of grasses. Tall grasses provide a safe home for countless insects, birds, and little mammals. When you walk in a grassy meadow to collect grasses, watch for nests and burrows. Look closely for bugs. How many different kinds can you find?

At night, you will see fireflies like tiny lanterns in the grass. The male firefly is the one in the air, flashing his green or yellow light on and off to attract a female. When the female on the ground finds a male that she takes a shine to, she flashes back. Different species of fireflies have different signals. Each species has its own pattern of flashes and pauses. When a female is hungry, she copies the pattern of another species of firefly to trick the male into coming to her. Then she eats him!

Children have always loved—and probably always will love—to catch fireflies. Catch them gently with your hands, and put them in a glass jar with holes punched in the lid. When your jar looks like a flashing lantern, set it down in the grass to see if the little lights attract other fireflies. Release the fireflies before you go to bed.

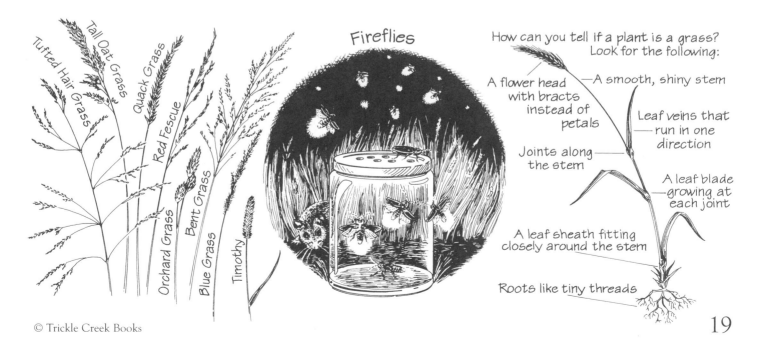

Tufted Hair Grass

Tall Oat Grass

Quack Grass

Red Fescue

Orchard Grass

Bent Grass

Blue Grass

Timothy

Fireflies

How can you tell if a plant is a grass? Look for the following:

A flower head with bracts instead of petals

A smooth, shiny stem

Leaf veins that run in one direction

Joints along the stem

A leaf blade growing at each joint

A leaf sheath fitting closely around the stem

Roots like tiny threads

Summer EcoJournal

_____

_____

_____

_____

_____

_____

_____

_____

_____

June 20: Early this morning, I walked in the woods while the dew was still heavy on the ground. The steamy green atmosphere and knee-high ferns reminded me of a tropical rainforest. Monkey vines, bittersweet, and thick poison ivy wound around and around tree trunks and branches the way strangler figs do in a tropical forest. Tiny white flowers on the privet shrubs added a full, sweet fragrance to the morning air. Just as I was imagining myself in a lush tropical rainforest, I heard the call of a woodpecker—an eerie whinny of notes exactly like some exotic bird in a jungle. For a moment, as I looked up through the layers of green above me, I half expected to see a monkey or a sloth or at least a poison arrow frog!

We may not have red and blue frogs in Pennsylvania, but we have salamanders. I love to look for them under damp leaves or logs. Their tiny four-toed feet look like little hands, and their colors and patterns are sometimes surprising. I once found a bright red salamander with deep red spots on its back and a yellow underbelly. (We later identified it as a newt in the red eft stage, the stage when the newt lives on land instead of in the water.) I was a teacher at the time, and I wanted to keep the little animal to show my class, but we were miles from home and needed a way to carry it. Salamanders need moisture. Even picking one up with dry hands can injure it. We finally found a little jar in the trunk of our car. It had originally held small red peppers called pimientos. When we put the red eft in the jar, it looked exactly right, like a little red pepper—only with feet!

Search for Salamanders

A salamander is a small animal that looks like a lizard but is really more like a frog. It is an *amphibian* with a soft moist skin, which shines almost like glass. Since salamanders are small and secretive and move quietly under the leaf litter on a forest floor, you may never have seen one. But once you know where to look, you can have fun searching for—and finding—them.

Salamanders like damp, shady places. They hide under cool rocks, old mossy logs, bark, or leaf litter. A good place to search for salamanders is near ponds or creeks, where most species breed. (Some salamanders spend their entire lives in water.) To look for woodland salamanders, carefully lift up a few logs or rocks, or dig down into a pile of moist leaves with your hands. You should uncover several kinds of salamanders. Remember to replace the logs and rocks in their original positions.

You can catch a salamander with your hands, but be as gentle as possible. If you grab a salamander, it may lose its tail, although many kinds of salamanders can grow another. When you catch a salamander, study it closely. How long is it? What color is it? (You may be surprised!) Is it striped or dotted? How many toes does it have? Do you see gills, grooves around the sides of the body, or a fold under the throat?

It's fun to keep a salamander in a terrarium for awhile, but you will need to consider how to keep it comfortable. Put layers of damp leaves in the bottom of the terrarium. Provide a small, mossy log, and keep it moist. Keep the terrarium in a shady place, a humid place if possible. Feed the little animal earthworms, insects, insect eggs and larvae, and bits of beef or other meat. Salamanders are entirely *carnivorous*, or meat-eating. If you put live insects in the terrarium, watch carefully to see how the salamander catches them with its long tongue.

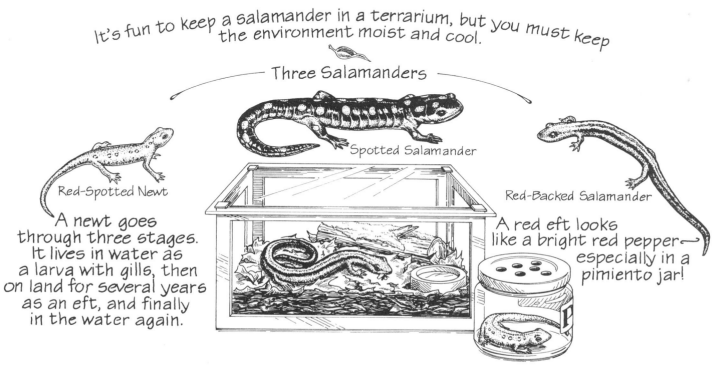

It's fun to keep a salamander in a terrarium, but you must keep the environment moist and cool.

Three Salamanders

Spotted Salamander

Red-Spotted Newt

A newt goes through three stages. It lives in water as a larva with gills, then on land for several years as an eft, and finally in the water again.

Red-Backed Salamander

A red eft looks like a bright red pepper—especially in a pimiento jar!

Summer EcoJournal

_____

_____

_____

_____

_____

_____

_____

June 30: My daughter Sandi and her husband Jim live near us on the other side of the woods. Sandi is my best friend—she was even as a child. We often do things together. Today we went to a country market to buy shrubs and flowers. As we walked between rows of little trees and boxes of bright flowers, Sandi spotted a cat among the plants. Sandi finds cats wherever we go. When she was little, we would return from a trip to the beach or a day at an amusement park, excited by the events of the day. While the rest of the family discussed the big waves or the Super Dooper Looper, Sandi would report, "I found a yellow and white kitten and fed it some ice cream." If she thought a cat was a stray, she would try to talk us into taking it home. She did it to me today!

Other shoppers walked between the shrubs without noticing the black and white cat hiding under one of them. But Sandi knelt down to call the cat and he came to her right away, pushing his head against her and purring. When she lifted him up, he hung like a wet towel over her shoulder. "Oh, he's *skinny*," she said. And he was. His back bones and shoulder and hip bones stuck out at odd angles, and his head looked enormous on his long lean body. Sandi and Jim already have two cats, so she decided that I would have to take this one. "He's beautiful, Mom," she urged. He was black with prim white feet and a cockeyed white muzzle. "And he needs a home!"

We checked with the market employees and they agreed that he needed a home. The cat had been with them for a week, looking even more starved when he turned up than he did now. We checked with Bob and, surprisingly, he agreed that we could bring him home. So we did!

How to Tail a Snail

Snails are fascinating little animals, which carry their homes on their backs. They can withdraw their soft bodies into their spiral-shaped homes for protection. Some can even slam the door—a disk called the *operculum*—or seal the opening shut. As the snail grows, its home grows too, adding coil upon coil to the open end of the shell.

There are more than 40,000 different species of snails and slugs throughout the world. (Snails have shells. Slugs don't.) They occur almost everywhere. Snails can be found on land or up in trees, in freshwater ponds and creeks, or in saltwater shallows or depths. If you look for snails, you will probably find the familiar garden snails or pond snails. On land, look closely at the leaf litter on a damp forest floor or in moist, shady areas in your yard or garden. Look for "snail tracks," glistening mucus trails on leaves and rocks. The snail's single foot has glands that pour out a slimy substance that enables the snail to move easily—but very slowly—over any surface. In fresh water, look for snails on pond weeds or blades of grass.

An interesting way to attract snails is to provide a cool daytime habitat for them. Set a terracotta flowerpot on its side in a damp, shady area of your garden. Check the flowerpot each day to see if any snails are seeking shelter there. When you find a snail, make a tiny mark on its shell with a colored marker or a dab of paint. Continue to check the flowerpot each day. Do the same snails return to the flowerpot after feeding each night? Are snails creatures of habit? Try moving the flowerpot at night, when the snails aren't there, to a nearby location. What happens?

You can easily keep *pond* snails in an aquarium with water plants. Look for snail eggs—lines of jelly on the underside of leaves. Gently, carefully, look at the eggs through a magnifying lens each day to watch the tiny snails grow! Keep *garden* snails in a terrarium with a lid. Make sure their environment is moist and cool. Give them vegetable fish food, water, and soft fat. Examine the fat with a magnifying lens to see tiny snail tooth marks!

To tail a snail, follow its trail.

Summer EcoJournal

Dragonfly

Bumblebee

Firefly

Common Blue

Walkingstick

Grasshopper

Question Mark

Ladybug Beetle

July 5: The black and white cat was wildly frightened in the car and then spent two days hiding under a bed. But now he's named (we named him Charlie), fed (he's already less bony), and beginning to explore the house (Bailey is not happy). Charlie loves to cuddle. He jumps into my lap and puts his front paws on my shoulders, purring like a small engine. Bailey watches from a distance and won't meet my eyes. Charlie sleeps with us at night while Bailey is hunting in the moonlight. When Bailey is ready to come in, he doesn't dart into the house like a white streak. Instead he sits several feet from the door and waits for me to carry him into the house. He hisses at Charlie when they pass each other. Bailey is telling us in a hundred ways how hurt he is that we have brought an intruder-cat into his house.

This morning, low cat growls woke us early. But we didn't mind after all, because in the cool, pale morning light, we saw the first fawns of the summer. Two tiny speckled fawns stayed close to their mother as she browsed at the edge of the lawn. Their baby faces are shortened and their eyes and ears are big. They are richly colored—red-brown and white. One fawn nuzzled the doe, trying to nurse, but she kept stepping away. The other fawn was playful and skittish. The doe's brother was with them, too. We called him the Martian buck when his growing antlers looked like unearthly knobs, but now his antlers are branching. Each antler is about ten inches high with two prongs at the top. What is he growing?

24

Praying Mantis

How to Track and Capture BUGS

In summer, the world is full of insects and spiders and millipedes and centipedes. Summer nights ring with insect music and bug buzz. Lazy summer afternoons are disturbed by tiny flying missiles—stinging, humming bug bombs. But where are all those bugs when you want them?

An easy way to collect bugs is to make a bug trap. Then you can observe bugs closely, take photos or make sketches, perhaps keep them for a day or two, and then release them. To make a great bug trap, choose a small container without a lid, such as a margarine dish or a small jar. Dig a hole in the ground in a flower bed or patch of weeds or grass. Place your container in the hole, so that the top is just below the level of the ground. To keep rain out of the container, cover it with a piece of wood supported by four stones. Put some soil and leaves in the bug trap for the bugs to shelter in and a piece of apple or cheese for bait. Check the bug trap each morning to see who dropped in!

Of course, you can attract bugs with bits of food almost anytime or anywhere. Try putting out sugar water, a tiny piece of raw meat, and a bite of fruit. Watch and record which insects and other creatures eat each kind of food. You can also attract bugs by providing a cozy shelter. The flowerpot that you put out for snails during the day (*see "How to Tail a Snail" on page 23*) may fill up with daddy longlegs at night.

If you want to be a *serious* bug tracker, try stalking a cricket by following the song the male makes by rubbing its wings together. Listen for the cricket's loud chirp. Then walk softly toward the sound until you think you're very near the cricket. Can you locate it? Use a flashlight if you're stalking after dark.

If you're *really* serious, try looking for bug tracks. First collect tiny tracks, so that you know what they look like. Spread fine chalk dust on a sheet of black construction paper. Catch some bugs and carefully set them down on the paper. What kind of tracks do they leave? Ant tracks are complicated patterns, most beetle tracks are wavy parallel lines, and millipede tracks are beautiful wavy lines.

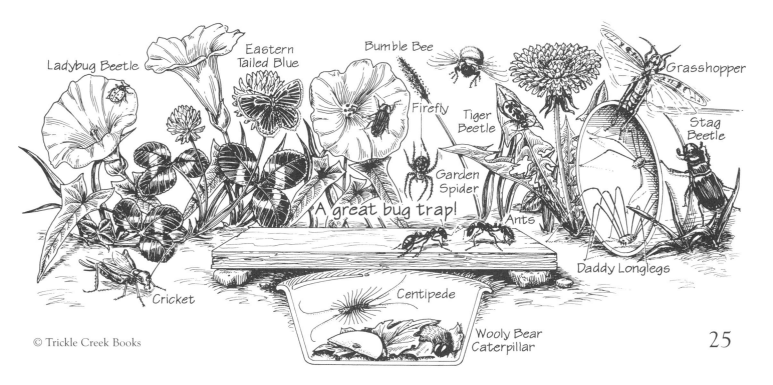

Summer EcoJournal

July 8: Sandi and I took a favorite walk that takes us by a large green pond. We stopped to watch a wood duck with her nine ducklings. The brown-feathered ducks are about half as big as their mother. They are such accomplished followers that they looked silly and made us laugh. When the mother goes up on the bank, all of the ducklings go up on the bank. When she goes back in the water, they all go back in the water. When she swims around a cattail, they all swim around a cattail.

Suddenly, as we stood watching the ducks, something whizzed by us, plopped into the water, and disappeared. At first, we thought it was another duck, but it didn't reappear. The tiny duckweed plants that cover the pond were undisturbed. There wasn't a ripple. Then we saw a small brown animal on the other side of the pond. Its ratlike tail rose above the water and curled over its body like a scorpion's. It was a muskrat.

Another muskrat with shining, dense fur came out of a burrow dug into the bank of the pond. The two muskrats slipped into the water, and like escorts, swam on either side of the wood duck with her line of ducklings. Thinking that the muskrats might eat the baby ducks, Sandi couldn't bear to watch. But the ducks weren't alarmed. They swam past the muskrats without even looking at them. Muskrats mostly eat plants, especially the tender roots and stems of cattails. We watched the muskrats for a long time. They were active and interesting and beautiful in the water.

26

Explore a Pond

A pond is a lively world of plants and animals that thrive at every level of the water—from the quiet surface to the mud at the bottom. But ponds have become a vanishing habitat, choked with garbage and filled in by developers. Even common frogs are disappearing, perhaps because of too much pollution. As you learn to explore a pond, look for signs of health or stress. Watch for changes. Try to think of ways that you could help protect the pond, perhaps by getting your neighborhood or community interested in caring for it.

A good time to approach a pond is at dawn. Sit down quietly in tall grass or behind dense shrubs where you can't be seen. Listen for the first morning sounds made by birds, frogs, and insects. Watch for animal visitors to the pond. Begin exploring the pond by walking slowly around it. Look for small paths and tracks along the muddy shore. Can you identify them? Look for plants growing in or on the water. You may see tall cattails with long, narrow leaves and brown flower spikes that look like cigars. If you see pond lilies with round, floating leaves, look for frogs and insects that might be resting on them. The pond may look green with slimy, stringy algae or with a carpet of tiny round duckweed plants (a favorite food for ducks). Check the stems of plants growing at the edge of the water for the outgrown skins of water insects.

Watch for birds that nest, shelter, or feed at ponds. You might see a big-headed kingfisher dive into the water after a fish. Or you could spot a green heron, a wood duck, or a mallard. Along the shallow edges of the pond, look for fish, tadpoles, newts, and water beetles. Use a small dip net to catch some pond critters, and then put them in a bucket of pond water. Observe them closely with a magnifying lens. Look for pond snails on plants or hanging upside down along the underside of the water surface. Watch for insects that walk on water, like the water striders, or insects that swim, like backswimmers. Pull your net or a wire sieve through the mud at the bottom to catch bottom dwellers: a clam, a crayfish, a leech, or insect larvae. Then return the critters to the pond or keep them for awhile in an aquarium. (*See "Keep a Creek Aquarium," on page 33. Also, read page 5 for tips on water safety.*)

Never explore a pond alone. It's more fun with a friend anyhow!

Cattails · Dragonfly · Female Mallard · Iris · Green Frog · Fisher Spider · Water Strider · Duckweed · Tadpoles · Pond Lilies · Backswimmer · Pond Snail · Painted Turtle · Diving Beetle · Sunfish · Minnow · Newt · Dragonfly Larva · Crayfish · Horse Leech · Clam

Summer EcoJournal

July 11: Today we accomplished one rescue and failed at another. Bailey caught a woodland jumping mouse, a gorgeous little creature with a white belly, a white-tipped tail, and bright orange fur. When we saw that the mouse was alive, we rushed toward Bailey and surprised him into dropping it. A jumping mouse is like a miniature kangaroo. It has big hind legs and a ridiculously long tail that enable it to leap wildly into the air and land ten feet away! As soon as the jumping mouse was free of Bailey's mouth, it bounced three feet straight up into the air. Then it bounded away like a reckless performer on a pogo stick. Bailey didn't even try to pursue the mouse. He was probably exhausted from catching it in the first place.

Later in the day, Bob brought a slender, black and white checkered snake to show me. He held the little milk snake, which was not much bigger than a pencil, behind its head. The snake's body was concealed inside Bob's hand. When I asked him where he had found the milk snake, he answered, "In the birdhouse where the wrens are nesting. Look!" He lifted the snake up as evidence. As the tiny snake was suspended from Bob's fingers, we could see the outline of four tiny bird's eggs in its belly. It looked like a ripe string bean! Of course we were sorry that the wrens had lost their eggs—there was a silly urge to pinch the eggs up the length of the snake and out of its mouth—but baby snakes have to eat, too, I guess.

28

Grow a Gourd House for a Bird

Although gourds aren't usually eaten, they have been grown for thousands of years. People have made spoons and dippers, cups and bottles, musical instruments, and toys from gourds. You might like to grow gourds to make birdhouses, or "gourd houses." Wrens, tree swallows, and purple martins especially like homes made of gourds.

Gourds are planted in late April or May after the danger of frost is past. Buy bottle gourd seeds (*Lagenaria siceraria*) rather than a package of mixed gourd seeds. Form small hills of soil about six feet apart in full sun. Then plant four or five seeds about an inch deep in each hill. The gourd plants can climb on a fence or trellis, or they can grow along the ground. If your gourds lie on the ground as they grow, you can put wood shavings or straw on the ground, so that the gourds won't get spots on them. The gourds can be harvested from late August into October—when they are very hard to the touch and when the little curly stem, or *tendril*, next to each gourd withers. When you cut the gourds from the vine, leave several inches of stem on each one.

Hang the gourds out of the sun to dry until you can hear the seeds rattle inside when they are shaken. Drying may take several weeks or months. Clean any mold from the gourds by scraping them with a table knife or scrubbing them with steel wool. Decide exactly where the entrance hole will go and mark it with a pencil. Make sure the hole is not so high on the gourd that it will let in rain or so low that baby birds could fall out! Then ask an adult for help in drilling a beginning hole and finishing the hole with a keyhole saw. Make a small hole, 1 inch to 1½ inches in diameter, to attract wrens or tree swallows. Make a larger hole, 2½ inches, for purple martins. (To attract martins, you must hang a large collection of gourds.) Shake the dried seeds and pulp out of the hole.

To finish the gourd house, drill several holes in the bottom of the gourd for drainage and two holes at the top for hanging. If you paint the gourd house with varnish, it will last for several years. Hang it from a branch by threading a cord or wire through the holes at the top.

A gourd house makes a cozy home for wrens, but like other birdhouses, it can be entered by snakes.

After eating four wren eggs, a baby milk snake looks just like a ripe string bean.

Summer EcoJournal

July 16: Our grandchildren—Nathan, who is eleven, and Kayla, ten,—arrived yesterday from Colorado to spend three weeks with us. Now that the children are here, the summer days take on an added glow of happiness and fun. There are so many things we want to do together.

Today we went swimming in the Yellow Breeches Creek. It's a wide, rippling creek, shaded by tall trees. The water is transparent. You can see smoothly rounded pebbles and mossy rocks on the bottom—or if you're lucky, a speckled brook trout darting through the shadows. We took a small net to catch creek critters and a shallow plastic tray to keep them in. First we found snails, shiny minnows, and empty mussel shells. Then as we turned rocks over, we discovered miniature monsters (insect larvae) and tiny structures made of pebbles and sticks (caddisfly cases).

Nathan wanted to catch crayfish. The more he looked for them, the more he found them. We decided we were wading in a "crawfish bed." When he scooped one up with the net, *he* was the one who was hooked! While Nathan and Bob chased crawdads, Kayla and I waded downstream to look for creek weeds for my water garden. We found a long flowing water grass and a bog plant with purple orchid-like flowers. When we returned, Nathan had mastered the skill of catching crawdads. He would locate one hiding under a rock, remove the rock, and swoop down with the net *behind* the crayfish. When crayfish are in danger, they snap their tails down and shoot through the water backwards. We had a family debate about whether to put the crawfish in Trickle Creek or the pond, finally deciding to release them. They're more fun to catch than to keep.

30

Creek Critters

Is there a kid in the world who can resist a creek? There seems to be an irresistible urge to pick up a smooth creek rock and throw it into the water. Or to try to catch a minnow with your bare hands. Or to take off your shoes and wade. Or to "accidentally" fall in, so that you might as well splash and play for awhile before you get out.

The next time you feel the magic of a creek pulling you into the water, be prepared to really explore it. Wear old sneakers, so that you can wade without slipping or hurting your feet. Take a small, fine-mesh net and a plastic pail, and plan on collecting creek critters. Put some creek water and water weeds in the pail. Then it will make a fine temporary home for the critters you collect.

Stand downstream—facing the current—to keep from muddying the water and making it too cloudy to see what's in it. Be still for a minute to get used to looking into the water. What do you see? Rocks? Water weed? Minnows? Is that all? If you spend an hour collecting critters, you will teach yourself to spot things that you never noticed before. Lift a good size rock out of the water and look at the underside. You may find snails, worms, insect larvae (strange, wiggly things), or water bugs. Don't try to pick them off the rock, because you would probably hurt them. Try swishing the rock with the critters through the water in your pail to wash them into the pail.

When you pick up a rock from the creek bed, look quickly to see if anything moves out from under it—tiny fish that dart to another sheltering rock or crayfish that look like miniature lobsters. Use your net to catch them. Then gently turn the net inside out in the pail of water, so that the critters can swim out of the net into the pail. Another way to collect critters from a creek is to slowly drag the net through the water until you catch something. Then release it in the pail. While you're collecting creek critters, don't forget to look up once in awhile. You don't want to miss an interesting bird or turtle or some other animal. (*See page 5 for tips on water safety.*)

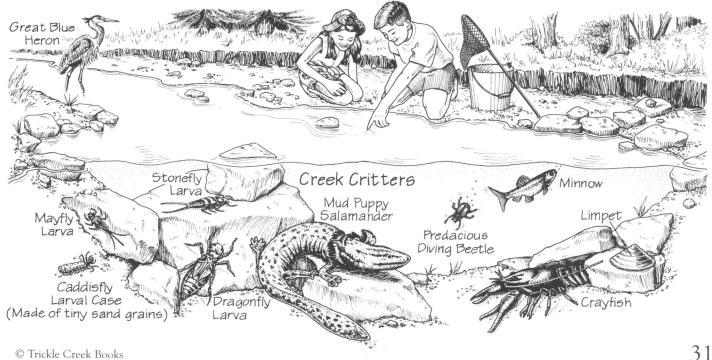

Great Blue Heron

Stonefly Larva

Creek Critters

Mud Puppy Salamander

Minnow

Mayfly Larva

Limpet

Predacious Diving Beetle

Caddisfly Larval Case (Made of tiny sand grains)

Dragonfly Larva

Crayfish

Summer EcoJournal

_____

_____

_____

_____

_____

_____

_____

_____

_____

_____

_____

July 17: By mid-morning, we knew this would be one of those oppressive summer days when the temperature and the humidity compete to see which will be the first to reach 100. The sky was white with haze, and the heat forced itself on us like hot air rushing out of an oven. We all agreed that we should spend another day in the cold-water creek. This time we would go tubing.

We rounded up four oversized inner tubes, a thermos of lemonade, and a length of rope. At the creek, we tied the thermos to one of the tubes and then tied all the tubes together, so that they would float in a line—like the wood ducklings. We spent four hours tubing down the Yellow Breeches, sometimes floating lazily, sometimes tumbling and tangling through white water, and sometimes swimming and diving while one person kept the tubes.

It always fascinates me to explore a creek from the water rather than from the bank. We were in the center of activity. Kayla pointed to a large painted turtle soaking up heat on the creek bank. Nathan spotted the head of a small water snake as it swam across the current directly in front of us. We saw mallard ducks paddling in the shallows, a kingfisher diving for its lunch, swallows fluttering like moths, and a green heron posing on an overhanging branch. A great blue heron with an enormous wingspan flew downstream. We found a cavity dug into a clay bank with white eggs in it! It must have been the nest of a bank swallow. What a perfect way to spend a steamy summer day!

Keep a Creek Aquarium

With care, you can keep your creek critters in an aquarium, where you can easily observe them. By including gravel and plants as well as animals, you will create a fascinating freshwater ecosystem in your aquarium.

Begin by scrubbing a glass aquarium and rinsing it well with clean water. If you have an undergravel filter, fit it in place. Collect some gravel, sand, and rocks from a creek, including a couple of "mossy" rocks that have vegetation on them. Rinse the gravel, sand, and rocks before putting them in the aquarium. Arrange them so that the ground level slopes. Then you will have shallow water and deeper water in the aquarium—just the way critters like it! This is a good time to position a bubbler (a pump and aerator) in the aquarium, too.

Collect or buy water plants, and place them in the aquarium. Anchor their roots by heaping gravel over them. To keep from disturbing your arrangement, lay a sheet of newspaper over the plants and gravel before slowly adding creek water. Then remove the paper. Leave the aquarium alone for several days while the water "settles."

Before adding creek critters, turn on the bubbler to create a "current" in the water and to add oxygen to the water. Animals and plants that thrive in fast-flowing creeks need plenty of oxygen. They can't survive in still water. Finally, add the critters—minnows, crayfish, water insects and larvae, mussels, and snails—to your aquarium. Keep the aquarium out of direct sunlight, but not in a dark place. Add a little fish food once a day and small bits of meat if you are keeping meat eaters, such as crayfish, mayfly larvae, or dragonfly larvae. You don't want to pollute the water with too much food, but don't be concerned about a little debris on the bottom. Snails and mussels will help take care of it.

A lively aquarium is more fun to watch than television!

Bubbler and filter

Sloped gravel

Air pump

Use newspaper to protect plants and gravel when you add water.

Summer EcoJournal

_____

_____

_____

_____

_____

_____

_____

_____

July 18: Early this morning, we hiked on a nature trail at a nearby park. The trail is only a mile long, but it winds through a remarkable variety of habitats. The path begins at a lively pond, continues into a deep shady woods, weaves through a sunny tall-grass meadow, follows the banks of the Yellow Breeches Creek, and finally returns through a bog to the pond. I love this trail, because you never know what you might see. I once saw a mink slip out of the brush directly in front of me!

We enjoyed seeing bright birds and wildflowers along the trail, but the biggest hit was the wineberries. Growing along the shady creek, the berry bushes were fresh and unwilted in the heat. Maybe they were dipping their roots into the water. Wineberries, which are related to wild raspberries and blackberries, are a clear wine-red color, juicy and plump. The bushes look like other wild berry bushes, with quilted leaves and long canes, but the berries grow differently. Immature wineberries grow inside hairy brown husks, which open to reveal the luscious berries. The best and biggest berries are deep inside the bush. As you reach for the berries, the bush reaches for you! It embraces you with its long arms and wicked thorns, so that you can't retreat without tearing and scratching your skin.

We nibbled on berries along the nature trail, but when we were home again, we decided to do some serious berry picking. We showed Nathan and Kayla where to find wineberries in the woods. After an hour, our fingers were stained with berry juice, our arms were tattooed with scratches, and our legs were dotted with insect bites, but we had berries! We sugared them generously and ate them on heaps of vanilla ice cream.

Make Sun Tea and Mint Lemonade

Hot chocolate in a warm mug is wonderful on a cold wintry day. And fresh apple cider is delicious in the fall. But there is nothing in the world like a frosted glass of ice cold tea or lemonade on an oven-hot summer day. You can even use the sun to brew the tea for you! To make sun tea, fill a quart jar with cold water and four or five tea bags. Set the jar outside with a lid on it in full sun for several hours. After the tea has slowly brewed in the sun, add sugar, lemon, and ice. Enjoy!

To make more exciting summer drinks, try growing your own fresh mint—or even a collection of mints. For example, you could plant spearmint, peppermint, lemon mint, water mint, wild mint, apple mint, and mountain mint. Many mints grow wild, but since you will be growing your mint for food, you should buy the plants at a nursery to be safe. Mint is very easy to grow—actually, it grows *too* well. A few small plants will spread like wildfire and take over an entire flower bed in no time. If you want to keep your mint in a small area, you'll need to put something underground to confine its roots and runners. You can make an underground "fence" by burying thin strips of wood or metal several inches in the ground around the plant. Or simply plant the mint in a large pot with holes in the bottom for drainage, and bury the entire pot in the ground. *Then* the mint won't be able to get out!

Once the mint is established and looks green and healthy, you can pick leaves from it all summer without hurting it. Add washed mint leaves to your sun tea while it brews in the sun, or make pure mint tea with mint leaves but without tea bags. Add fresh mint leaves to cold lemonade for a new flavor. Experiment with different combinations of tea, lemon, sugar, and mint. Create a new refreshing summertime drink!

Mint smells good and tastes good. So does sun tea!

Spearmint

Most mints have square stems, and leaves that are opposite each other.

Peppermint

Unless you confine it, mint will spread like wildfire.

Summer EcoJournal

July 22: Sandi and Jim took the kids to Hershey Park today. When they came home just before dusk, we welcomed them with a big picnic supper. Bob had grilled a long piece of salmon. Before serving it, he removed a ten-inch length of fat smoky skin from the fish, and Kayla took it out to the compost pile. We all agreed that the fish skin would surely attract some hungry animals.

After dinner, we continued sitting at the picnic table as night fell. An orchestra of insects tuned up their instruments with shrill chirps and buzzes. The concert began with sudden force and filled the summer night with insect songs. The air cooled, and a shy breeze stirred the leaves in first one tree and then another. Dark pine trees loomed above us and blocked most of the stars from our view. We talked quietly. All the while, the fish skin lay on the compost pile, fat and smoky and tantalizing.

Every so often, someone would walk to the end of the deck and check on the compost pile. Finally the report came that a big opossum was circling the pile with its nose held high and working overtime. None of us was interested enough to move from the table. Then Nathan announced that a fox was approaching the compost pile. Now, a fox is worth getting up for. We rushed into the house and crowded around a window to watch. Bailey jumped between us to sit on the window sill. He probably knows that fox! Another fox trotted out of the darkness. The opossum retreated but came back again. One fox snatched the fish hide, and holding it high, disappeared into the night. The possum left with a piece of watermelon. The second fox walked away without looking back. Nathan said, "I *knew* that fish skin would work!"

Plan a Low-Trash Picnic

Think of all the people who enjoy picnics in the summertime. Think of all the TRASH that is generated by picnics—just when landfills are overflowing, litter is covering our natural areas, and plastic waste is piling up. Don't you wish we could do something about these problems?

Try planning a low-trash—or no-trash—picnic. Think about what food and utensils you want to take on your picnic. Then consider how you could eliminate all of the throwaway items. Here are some suggestions:

Use a lunch box or picnic basket instead of a paper or plastic bag.

Use reusable plastic plates, cups, forks, spoons, and knives (the kind you can wash and use again).

Use a fabric napkin instead of a paper one.

Bring your drink in a thermos or reusable container. Drink from the thermos lid or a reusable cup. Don't use plastic foam cups.

Pack sandwiches, chips, and other food in reusable containers rather than carrying them in plastic bags or plastic wrap.

Use an empty peanut butter jar to hold fruit or salad.

Put leftover food on your compost pile.

In the United States, the average family produces more than one hundred pounds of trash each week! If we don't stop generating so much garbage, the earth will become a huge garbage dump. We need to think about everything we buy and everything we own in a new way, asking ourselves, "Can this be reused, repaired, or recycled?" This is a way to care for our Earth.

Of all the bugs in the world, the one that bothers me the most is a litterbug.

Try to leave a wild place just the way you found it or better!

Summer EcoJournal

_____

_____

_____

_____

_____

_____

_____

_____

_____

_____

_____

July 25: We were outside on the deck when Bailey came trotting across the lawn looking self-conscious. Kayla cried, "Bailey's got a little yellow bird!" I started to shout, "See if you can catch him," but Nathan was already running. Bailey halted and crouched low, perhaps waiting to see what was coming—praise or fury. He decided it wasn't praise and streaked towards the woods, still holding his prey. Nathan launched forward in a flying tackle, missed "the white streak," but recovered the dropped bird.

Only it wasn't a bird. It was an imperial moth, a large yellow moth as big as my hand. Even dead and tattered, it was beautiful. The moth had a sturdy yellow body with rosy markings and wide yellow wings with splotches and splatterings of soft colors—rose and lavender and gray. Moths usually hide and rest during the day, so that we don't often get to see them. I kept thinking about moths all day, wondering which spectacular moths might be hiding nearby. I couldn't wait for night to come. I planned to watch moths. Nathan and Kayla were planning to watch a video.

As soon as it grew dark, I went outside and tacked a sheet over the sliding glass door that opens onto the deck. I set up a floor lamp inside the house, so that it shined through the sheet. Every few minutes, I slipped outside to see what was crawling on the sheet. There were beetles and gnats and a few small gray moths, nothing very interesting. And I missed the end of the video.

38

Attract Moths with a Shining Sheet

You've probably noticed bright colored butterflies since you were a small child, but you may not have seen very many moths. Most moths fly and feed at night. Many moths are hard to find even when they are resting during the day, because their drab colors are good camouflage. (Some moths fly by day and have brighter colors.)

Nectar-feeding moths are attracted to the sweet scents of certain flowers. They are the night-shift pollinators, after butterflies have worked the day shift. Unlike butterflies, which perch on flowers as they feed, moths hover over blossoms like little helicopters. Moths and butterflies are different at rest, too. Moths spread their wings sideways when they rest. Butterflies hold their wings together over their backs.

Butterflies and moths are usually fairly easy to tell apart when you have a chance to look closely. Moths have plump bodies and short, feathery antennae. Butterflies have slender bodies and long antennae with tiny knobs at the ends.

It's fun to attract moths with a shining sheet. Hang a white sheet over a clothesline or between two tree limbs. Set up a flashlight behind it, so that the light shines through the sheet. After dark on a warm summer night, sit quietly in front of the sheet. It's like watching a big screen television. The program is "Flying Creatures of the Night." See if you can identify the cast of characters with a field guide to insects.

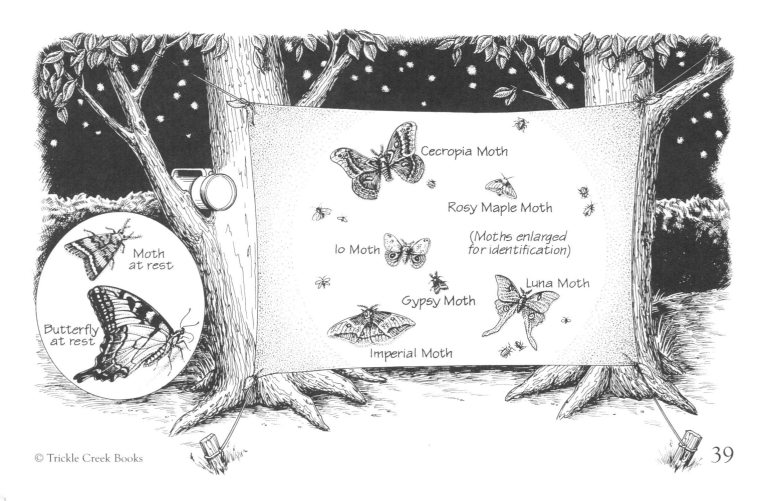

Moth at rest

Butterfly at rest

Cecropia Moth

Rosy Maple Moth

Io Moth

(Moths enlarged for identification)

Gypsy Moth

Luna Moth

Imperial Moth

Summer EcoJournal

August 1: After we returned from the airport, Bob and I took our lunch outside and ate without talking. We were so still that we could hear the tiny motor sound of the hummingbird as it hovered at the feeder. We could hear the sad sighing of the wind high in the pines. Bailey balanced on the deck railing, tail high. Charley peeked cautiously out the door. Abercrombie studied our every move, waiting for someone to offer him a bite of sandwich.

Bob said, "The cats are going to miss Nathan and Kayla. You know how they came up every night while we read together at bedtime."

I said, "Abercrombie will miss them too. All the petting and playing and extra attention they gave him. And Kayla is the only one who calls him 'Crumbles.' Now he's just Abercrombie again."

Bob said, "I'll miss them, too."

"I know," I said. "I will, too." And for a moment, the sad, sighing wind rose to a wail high in the pines.

40

You Can Be a Bee

When we admire flowers, we usually look at the colors and shapes of their petals. But the most interesting parts of a flower are in its center. That's where all the action is. The center of a flower is like a factory where seeds are quietly made. The trick is getting the male part of the flower—the yellow dust called *pollen*—to the tiny seeds-to-be in the female parts of the flower. Most flowering plants can't make seeds without "outside help." Bees, butterflies, and other insects, as well as birds, brush pollen onto the female parts of the flower as they land on the flower and move around. They act as *pollinators*. Even a breeze or water droplets can be pollinators. Even you can be a pollinator!

First you must be able to identify the parts of a flower. Choose a flower such as a lily, a pansy, or a cosmos. Use a magnifying lens to look closely at the stalk in the center of the flower. This is the *pistil*, or female part of the flower. Carefully open the pistil and look for the seeds-to-be, or *ovules*, at the bottom. Then look for slender stalks around the pistil. These are the *stamens*, the male parts of the flower. At the tip of each stamen is a tiny packet called an *anther*. When the anthers open, you can see the golden pollen inside. (Some plants don't have both male and female parts on the same flower. These flowers are called incomplete flowers.)

As a pollinator, you need to get pollen from the anther to the pistil. You can use a small paintbrush to gather the pollen. To do an interesting experiment, choose two plants of the same kind but of different colors—such as a yellow cosmos and a pink cosmos. Brush the pollen from a flower of one color onto the pistil of a flower of the other color. Take a photo of each of the "parent" plants, so that you can compare them to the new plant that grows from the seeds. Tag the flower that you pollinated and watch it until the flower fades and the petals fall. Shake the dried center of the flower over a plastic bag to collect the ripe seeds. Store the seeds in a covered jar in a cool place. Plant them next spring when the soil is warm. How do the flowers from the new plants compare to the parent plants?

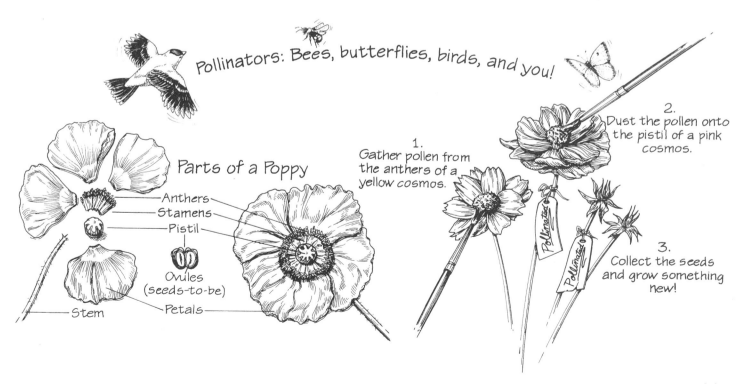

Pollinators: Bees, butterflies, birds, and you!

Parts of a Poppy

Anthers
Stamens
Pistil
Ovules (seeds-to-be)
Stem
Petals

1. Gather pollen from the anthers of a yellow cosmos.

2. Dust the pollen onto the pistil of a pink cosmos.

3. Collect the seeds and grow something new!

Summer EcoJournal

August 6: Once the children were gone, I slipped back into a regular routine of working and writing in my upstairs office. Sitting at the computer, I can look directly into the upper branches of a yellow pine. I often watch squirrels, blue jays, and woodpeckers—while I'm working, of course.

Four days ago, I realized that a pair of mourning doves are nesting in the pine. At first I didn't recognize their nest. It looked like a bundle of twigs, which might have scattered in a windstorm and lodged between two branches. But one day, I saw two fluffy whitish-gray birds lift their heads up from the messy twig pile. They were welcoming their mother (or father), who promptly fed them "pigeon milk." The little doves stick their beaks inside the parent's beak, prompting the adult to regurgitate a thick white milky-cereal stuff. The baby birds are fed this rich "milk" for nine days. It must be wonderful food, because I can see them growing each day. I have read that baby doves increase their weight thirty times in less than two weeks. This is going to be interesting to watch!

I've always loved the haunting call of the mourning dove. My father told me that when he first heard the mourning dove as a little boy, he thought it was the voice of God.

Help a Sloppy Mourner

As soon as we have a week of warm days in spring, the male mourning dove starts calling in a sweet, sad voice, "Coooo, cooooahhh, coo, coo." He courts the female by showing off in the air with fancy flight maneuvers. On the ground, he puffs out his throat, fans his tail, rushes at the female like an eager puppy, and then bows to her like a courtly gentleman. She, on the other hand, is very casual and seems more interested in preening her feathers. If she decides that he is the one for her, she places her beak trustingly in his. With their beaks locked, they bow together. If there are mourning doves in your area (they are found in every state), watch for this interesting courtship ritual.

Mourning doves don't nest in tree cavities or birdhouses. The male chooses a place for the nest, often next to the trunk of an evergreen or sometimes in a honeysuckle thicket or on the ground. His idea of how to build a nest is to place a four- or five-inch twig across a pair of branches. The female is charmed and immediately perches on the twig. Then the male brings more and more twigs, which she tucks under her. Even when both birds collect twigs and place them, they make a pretty sloppy nest. A strong wind is often disastrous to nesting mourning doves, because the baby birds can be blown out of the flimsy, open-air nests—or the loose nests can be blown away.

If you would like to help a sloppy mourning dove or a nest of little mourners, it's easy to build a nest cone for the birds. Use tin snips to cut a 12-inch square of window screening (¼-inch or ½-inch hardware cloth). Then trim the square to form a circle about 12 inches in diameter. Cut a pie-shaped wedge out of the circle and pull the two cut edges together so that they overlap. Wire the edges securely together. Fasten the nest with wire between two tree branches that are 6 to 16 feet above the ground. Then even in a fierce wind, the mourners can be glad!

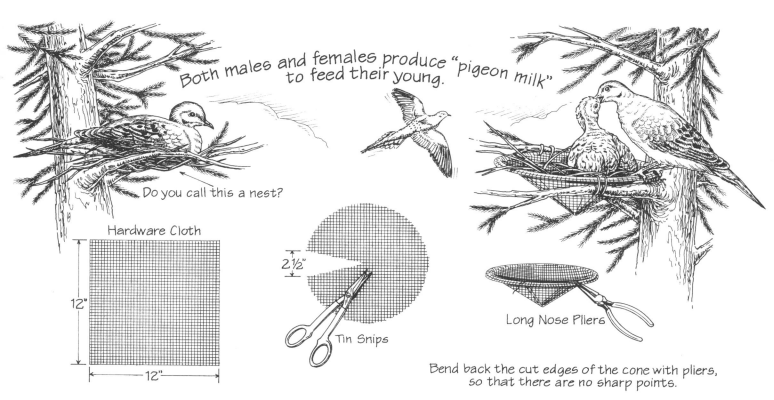

Both males and females produce "pigeon milk" to feed their young.

Do you call this a nest?

Hardware Cloth

12"

12"

2½"

Tin Snips

Long Nose Pliers

Bend back the cut edges of the cone with pliers, so that there are no sharp points.

Summer EcoJournal

August 15: My father is visiting us from Texas. We enjoyed watching the fawns come to the deer feeder with their mother. And we laughed when we surprised a baby groundhog cradling a watermelon rind at the compost pile. But even these beautiful babies weren't as much fun as the mushrooms.

We drove to Fuller Lake to hike. The lake was a dazzling green, reflecting sparks of sunshine from little waves. The forest in late summer is cloaked in deep green shadows. My dad veered off the trail, and we followed him into the shady, secret, steamy understory, where lush ferns grew on crumbling, mossy logs. The forest floor was carpeted with layers of damp leaves. We saw some familiar brown mushrooms, delicate and long-stemmed. Then we saw a large white mushroom. Suddenly we spotted mushrooms everywhere—a lemon-yellow mushroom with white scales and a white stem, a flat red mushroom on a curved white stem, a bright yellow mushroom with a pleated cap, a completely blue mushroom, a waxy green mushroom, leathery purple bracket mushrooms growing on a tree trunk, a sticky orange-yellow mushroom with branches like a coral, and a colony of tiny red, cuplike mushrooms. We seemed to be walking in an enchanted garden of colored mushrooms that popped up magically in front of our eyes. It was like walking in a Technicolor dream. I'd like to dream that again someday.

44

Make a Mushroom Spore Print

There is something almost magical about mushrooms. They seem to appear from nowhere, popping up overnight and then popping down again. Actually, a mushroom is only the fruit of a fungus. The true fungus is typically a tangle of fine threads, called a *mycelium*, which is found underground. The fungus fruit, or mushroom, contains spores, which are like tiny seeds that can produce more fungi and more mushrooms. The mushroom pops up out of the ground to spread the spores.

Mushrooms fascinate us because they come in so many different colors, shapes, and sizes. We wish we could make an interesting collection, but there is really no good way to preserve mushrooms. They can be dried, but their original colors and shapes will be lost in the process. The best way to collect mushrooms is to take photos or to make colored drawings.

You can also have fun making mushroom spore prints. Look for fresh, mature mushrooms in woods or meadows, especially after a rain. Look for mushrooms on fallen logs, standing dead trees, at the base of trees, under leaf litter, or right in a lawn! Pick two of each kind of mushroom you find, and carefully take them home in a basket—not in a bag, where they might get crushed or broken. Cut the stems off the mushrooms as close to the caps as possible. Then place one mushroom of each kind (gills down) on a sheet of white paper and one on a sheet of black paper. You won't know what color the spores are until they fall on the paper. Most spores are white, pink, dark yellow, or purplish black. The light spores will show up on black paper, and the dark ones will look great on white paper.

Place a bowl over each mushroom to keep the microscopic spores from blowing away. Leave the mushrooms in place overnight. Then gently remove the mushrooms from the paper and admire the gorgeous spore prints! If any mushroom didn't drop spores by morning, it was probably too young or too old. Try another. To protect your spore prints, cover them with clear contact paper or spray them from a distance of fifteen inches with a fixative.

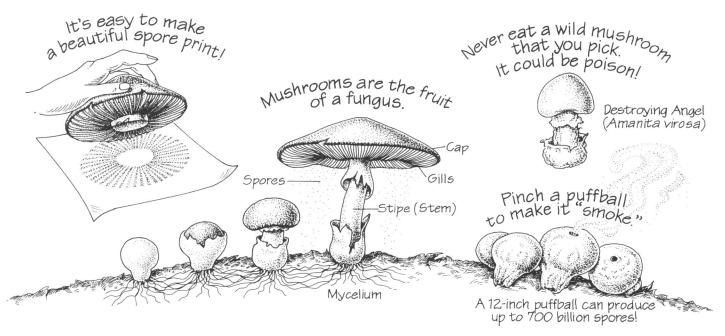

It's easy to make a beautiful spore print!

Mushrooms are the fruit of a fungus.

Spores

Cap

Gills

Stipe (Stem)

Mycelium

Never eat a wild mushroom that you pick. It could be poison!

Destroying Angel (Amanita virosa)

Pinch a puffball to make it "smoke."

A 12-inch puffball can produce up to 700 billion spores!

Summer EcoJournal

August 20: Day after day has been hot and humid. A white haze has blanketed the sky, and the heat has made me lazy. But today was cool. The sky was a clear sparkling blue, and the deep green shadows in the woods shimmered with vitality. In our family, we call these "October days" even when they're in August. They are days that call for a long walk.

I walked several miles along country roads, especially enjoying the wildflowers. Tall, weedy-looking chicory bloomed beside the road. The blue flowers are surprisingly delicate on their tough stalks and can't be picked because they immediately wilt. The sweet joe-pye-weeds stand taller than I am with their fuzzy clusters of pinkish-purple flowers. I saw fields of Queen Anne's lace (the wild carrot) with flowers crowded together like layers of lace doilies. The deep yellow goldenrods are already proclaiming the coming of fall, when _they_ will color the fields. Enormous purple thistles, "bull thistles," insist that summer is still here. It's quite an argument.

As I approached our house again, I saw a commotion in the distance. At first I thought it was Charlie, the black cat, in some kind of trouble, but, no, it was a shiny black crow—almost as big as a cat. The crow had found a small dusty spot in the lawn and was taking a dust bath. I've never seen a crow flopping on its back with its bald feet in the air. It made me laugh, and my voice sent the crow flying high into a tree, calling out a long loud protest.

46

Birds in Summer

August is a quiet month—a resting month—for most birds. Much of the flurry and hurry of nesting is over. It isn't time for them to migrate yet. There is an abundance of natural food. These are the lazy days for birds.

You might want to keep putting out some bird food at your bird feeders, because then the young birds will learn to visit your yard. Of course the birds won't be as interested in the feeders as they are during other seasons, because tasty fruits, seeds, and insects are plentiful. The most effective way to attract birds in August is to provide water for them. Not just water to drink, but water to bathe and play in! Watch what happens on a hot, dry day when you turn a sprinkler on. Do birds turn up? If you keep water outside in any container—a dishpan, a kiddie pool, a large bucket, even a garbage can lid—birds will find it and enjoy it. Then you can watch them drink and wade and splash.

Have you ever seen a dog roll on its back in the grass? Or a horse? (That's really something to see!) Well, birds also enjoy a dust bath, and you can help them by making a dust bowl. Clear an area two or three feet across by digging up all the vegetation growing there. Hollow out a shallow bowl in the ground and fill it with a mixture of fine sand and dirt. The dust bowl should be in the sun but close to shrubs or trees to give the birds cover. Once birds discover the dust bowl, they will flutter and roll and kick in the dust like a dog on the lawn. The dust probably helps control parasites that plague birds.

Another activity to enjoy in summer is to collect broken eggshells that you find scattered on the ground. (*Never* collect bird eggs from a nest.) Even fragments of shells are worth keeping, because they give an idea of the color, pattern, and size of the original egg. Bird eggshells are fragile and must be handled gently. Wash them carefully in warm soapy water, using a paintbrush to remove dirt. Store them on a bed of cotton in a small box.

Birds love to take a dust bath!

A garbage can lid makes a fine birdbath.

Bird eggshells are lovely and fun to collect.

Summer EcoJournal

August 24: This morning Bob and I, like any two dignified adults, lay down on our bellies at the edge of the lawn and lost ourselves in an alien world. Armed with magnifying lenses, we slowly explored the leaf-litter realm of tiny monsters. A bright red velvet mite with a clumsy, swollen body waded through dust on a leaf. We discovered a fuzzy web inside the center of a tiny flower. The web held ten perfectly round, clear eggs. A green worm crawled into view, so transparent that we could see a black spot inside it. A tiny slug with delicate antennae and beautiful markings slimed along a blade of grass that seemed as tall as a tree. A brown and gold millipede weaved over and under leaves and over and under twigs.

We gently pushed the leaf debris away until we had cleared what looked like a little plowed field. (It was really about six inches square.) The dirt was strewn with an empty snail shell, tiny acorn tops, wild cherry seeds, and other seeds. Earthworms, popping partly out of their holes and then quickly withdrawing, were an amazing sight! A spider web at the edge of our "field" was spangled with water droplets that reflected a rainbow of colors. A green inch worm arched and flattened like a strange dancer. What an odd place that magnified world was!

Safari to a World of Tiny Monsters

Some lazy day when you're looking for something to do, go on a safari in your backyard. Arm yourself with a magnifying lens, and take a beach towel or blanket to lie down on. Look for a moist area at the edge of the lawn where there is leaf litter. Make yourself comfortable—lie down on your stomach. Position your magnifying lens close to the ground, and enter a fantastic world of tiny monsters unlike anything you've ever seen!

Look for mighty millipedes, horrible mites with swollen red bodies, spider webs like fish nets, insects with huge inhuman eyes, caterpillars that lumber along like tanks, giant slugs with strange markings, and earthworms that poke their heads out of holes in the earth. As you explore further, gently move leaves and debris out of the way. Look for a monstrous snail or salamander. Look for insect eggs and fuzzy molds and mushrooms like slimy trees. Look and look until you lose yourself in this wonderful miniature world of monsters.

When you're ready to move on, choose other places to explore. Examine a sunflower with your magnifying lens. Sunflowers are usually crowded with insects among their petals. Peer into the centers of other flowers. Look under rocks or logs. (Then replace them in their original positions.) Study the bark of a tree. A magnifying lens is all the equipment you need to take you on an unforgettable hunting expedition—a safari—for tiny exotic beasts.

Summer EcoJournal

August 28: Today we saw a black locust explode in a blaze of light! In the late afternoon, a fierce thunderstorm developed. The sky grew suddenly dark, the trees began to bend and dance in the wind, and far-off peals of thunder boomed nearer and nearer like approaching cannons. We stood at a window watching the storm, when a shaft of lightning, a jagged discharge of pure electricity, swooped down upon a black locust tree with a shrieking, deafening crack. For a moment, the tree lit up, giving off light like a giant lantern. The trunk swelled and burst. Limbs and bark flew through the air in every direction. A shuddering explosion of thunder confirmed the attack.

We drew back from the window in alarm and waited for the storm to pass. In just a few minutes, the cannon booms receded, the trees grew quiet, and the rain stopped. We went out into the dripping woods to inspect the locust tree. The terrible expansion of the tree had deformed the trunk into a long donut shape. The trunk swelled out on either side of a large hole. We could see through the tree to the woods behind it. The dark, crosshatched bark lay strewn on the ground. Most of the branches had been torn off. The tree will surely die.

Locusts are not especially beautiful trees. Their limbs are scraggly and their trunks are often skinny. They're the last trees to get their leaves in the spring and the first to lose them in the fall. The locust has two redeeming features. It flowers in May with fragrant clusters of white blossoms, which hang like heavy bunches of white grapes. And its hard, strong wood is one of the best firewoods. We'll be grateful for the heat it gives next winter.

50

When You Know a Tree

There is something wonderful about really getting to know a tree. You see it with a new appreciation—even as a new and interesting friend. Choose a favorite tree to get to know, a tree outside your window or in your yard, a tree you like to climb, or a beautiful tree in a nearby park or woods. Ask an adult who knows about trees to identify the tree for you. Keep a scrapbook, a my-favorite-tree book, for at least a year.

Begin by taking the tree's measurements. To measure the *girth* of the tree (the distance around the trunk), wrap a tape measure around the tree at the standard height of five feet from the ground. The girth in inches will also give you a rough idea of the tree's age in years. Of course, a more accurate way to estimate the tree's age would be to count the annual growth rings on a stump of the same size and species as your tree. To find the size of the tree's *canopy*, or spreading branches, measure the distance from the trunk to the outermost branches in eight directions. Make a scale drawing in your scrapbook. Finally, to measure the height of the tree, walk 27 paces from the trunk. Ask a friend to hold a long stick upright at exactly that place. Walk three more paces away from the tree, lie down on your stomach facing the tree, and look past the stick to the top of the tree. Have your friend mark the stick where it crosses your line of sight as you look at the treetop. Measure the distance from the mark on the stick down to the ground. The height of the tree is ten times that distance. Repeat all of the measurements next summer to see how much your tree grows in a year.

You can study your tree's anatomy by collecting and preserving the leaves at different seasons, buds, blossoms, fruit, seeds, twigs, and bark. Don't remove bark from the tree (it will harm the tree), but "collect" bark by making a bark rubbing. Simply place a piece of paper against the bark and rub the side of a crayon back and forth to reveal the pattern of the bark. Save leaves and blossoms by pressing them, and preserve buds, seeds, and twigs by drying them. You can dry some fruits or dissect them and make a detailed drawing.

Observe your tree carefully and keep a record of birds and other animals that visit it, insect galls that grow on it, nests that are built in it, and weather damage. Take photos or make drawings at different seasons. When your scrapbook is full of observations and information, you will really know your tree. And to know a tree is to love it!

Summer EcoJournal

August 31: Summer is ending. All of the little wood ducks are grown, although they still swim in formation behind their mother. Their heads bob forward and back as if they have to work their way through the thick duckweed on the pond. The cattails are ripe and brown. Day and night, the air is filled with insect songs—tiny Japanese bells and rasping, sawing machines. (These are the sounds of autumn.) I pulled a thistle that had gone to seed. It expanded into silky, shimmering feathers and flew away. The grass in the wetland meadow is no longer golden. It is silvery now and somehow diminished. The grass is tilting and falling. It looks shorter.

Summer is ending. The leaves of the dogwoods are deep red, and the dogwood berries are ripe. Birds and squirrels are rushing to pick them. The lush emerald canopy of the woods is thinning, and the sun enters on a slant. Summer is ending.

Summer is ending, but I'm not ready for it to end. I never am, are you?

Celebrate Summer

Wade in a creek and catch creek critters.

Sleep under the stars in a sleeping bag.

Make a daisy chain.

Lie on your back and watch the clouds in a sunny sky.

Give a blackberry to a friend.

53

Wildlife Checklist

Use the checklist below to keep track of some of the animals you see. Record the date and place of your observations. Be patient. You probably won't spot all of the animals on the checklist this summer—or even this year!

	DATE	PLACE
CHORDATES - MAMMALS		
❏ Deer		
❏ Raccoon		
❏ Opossum		
❏ Skunk		
❏ Squirrel		
❏ Chipmunk		
❏ Groundhog		
❏ Fox		
❏ Rabbit		
CHORDATES - BIRDS		
❏ Robin		
❏ Cardinal		
❏ Blue Jay		
❏ Chickadee		
❏ Hawk		
❏ Crow		
❏ Duck		
❏ Owl		
CHORDATES - REPTILES		
❏ Turtle		
❏ Snake		
CHORDATES - AMPHIBIANS		
❏ Frog		
❏ Salamander		
ARTHROPODS - INSECTS		
❏ Beetle		
❏ Grasshopper		
❏ Firefly		
❏ Bumblebee		
❏ Cricket		
❏ Butterfly		
❏ Moth		
❏ Dragonfly		
❏ Praying Mantis		
❏ Walking Stick		
OTHER ARTHROPODS		
❏ Milipede		
❏ Spider		

Summer Butterflies

Can you imagine summer without butterflies? Why, it would be like a sky with no stars or a lake with no fish! But even during bright summer days—when colorful butterflies wander from flower to flower—we can't take them for granted. Butterflies suffer from the same careless human activities that harm other animals: pollution of air and water, wide use of insecticides and pesticides, and loss of habitat. Some kinds of butterflies are now rare. Some are endangered. Some have become extinct.

You can help provide habitat for butterflies by planting native plants that they like. Different butterflies require different kinds of plants. Use the illustrations below to help you choose plants that attract summer butterflies. If you want to learn to identify more butterflies, use a field guide to butterflies or insects. You can find one at your local library or bookstore.

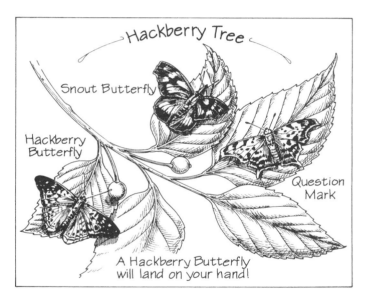

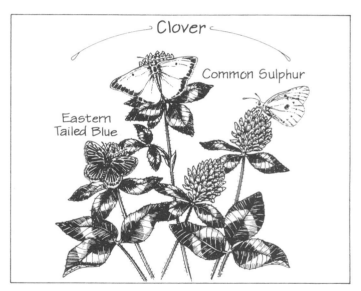

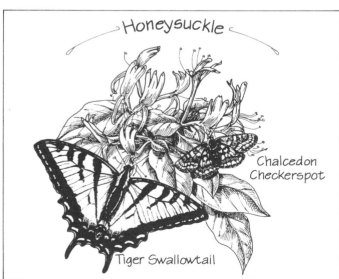

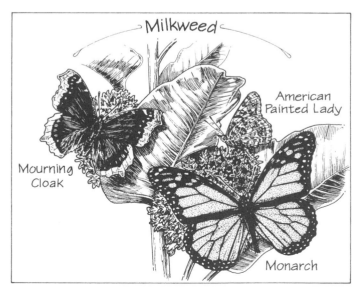

An EcoJournal for Every Season

You'll want to own all four of them.

Trickle Creek Books offers a series of four EcoJournals, one for each season, which are written by Toni Albert and illustrated by Margaret Brandt. All of the EcoJournals invite kids to explore the seasons with unusual nature activities and then to write about their experiences. The books include exquisitely illustrated writing pages for children, short entries from the author's nature journals that reflect her irrepressible delight in the natural world, and dozens of nature activities for children to try. Kids learn to develop a deep love and respect for the environment.

Here are some of the activities that are found in the other EcoJournals:

A Kid's Spring EcoJournal

- Build a mole dome
- Make a track trap
- Raise a wild caterpillar or tadpoles
- Build an eco-pond
- Make wildflower crafts
- Plant a butterfly garden
- Build a wildlife blind

A Kid's Fall EcoJournal

- Collect leaf galls and raise the larvae
- Build a bat house
- Collect a spider web
- Dissect an owl pellet
- Make leaf prints
- Sprout an acorn
- Take a sock walk

A Kid's Winter EcoJournal

- Track animals in the snow
- Test the purity of snow
- Make an owl call
- Make woodpecker pizza and bird biscuits
- Make winter potpourri
- Make a snowman for the birds

Each EcoJournal sells for $9.95. Order from your bookseller, online bookseller, or directly from us.

Trickle Creek Books

500 Andersontown Road
Mechanicsburg, PA 17055-6055

Toll-free 24-hour telephone - 800-353-2791
Telephone - 717-766-2638 • **Fax** - 717-766-1343
Web site - www.TrickleCreekBooks.com • **E-mail** - tonialbert@aol.com

Satisfaction Guarantee - If you are not satisfied with your purchase for any reason, return books for full refund. Thanks for ordering.